Printed in Great Britain
by Amazon

45646303R10046

"Breaking the Earth"

By Patrick McLeod

Patrick McLeod is an American born poet who has lived much of his life in Essex. He is an art historian who has also worked in business and as a teacher of English Literature.

His extensive interests are reflected in this collection of poetry. Although landscape and a sense of place feature frequently, his range is wide and - quite characteristically - a spiritual undercurrent is evident in these poems.

ISBN: 979 8 3701 7320 2

"Tessera"

By Mark Harris

This book collects short poems written over the last decade drawn from an extensive body of work.

He takes inspiration from his own life, those he meets and from other artists including Frida Kahlo and Leonard Cohen.

ISBN: 979 8 3865 5491 0

Ariadne's Thread Publishing

ariadnesthreadpublishing@gmail.com

Also available from

Ariadne's Thread Publishing

"Catharsis "

By Mark Harris

In this book Mark Harris draws together poems written over the last decade exploring themes of love and connection.

He takes inspiration from his own life, those he meets and from other artists including Frida Kahlo and Leonard Cohen.

ISBN: 979 8 8398 5005 7

"Seasons of Poetry "

By Brenda Wells

In this debut collection of poetry, Brenda Wells looks at the natural and gradual movement of the seasons, the impact of change and the need for personal reflection and positivity.

The countryside is a major source of inspiration as are the vicissitudes of life, also writers such as Emily Dickinson, Robert Frost, Laurie Lee and Jackie Morris.

ISBN: 979 8 3524 9864 4

The Beating Heart Metaphor

Here I spoke
Heartfelt words
A brief confession;
How I wished things could be.

Here I gazed
At a foreign shore
And a distant smile
Through rose tinted hours.

Here I unfurled myself
And tried to fill
An empty space
On an inner sea.

Here surf broke
Over expectation
As I battled the tide
And dared to dream.

Here ozone scents
Mixed with rain
As hope departed
In lamentation.

Here a seagull mourns
As sunlight fades
And footprints
Concede to rolling waves.

Yolk

Desire exposed
I clasp her knees in supplication
Praying she will part herself for me.

But it is she that eats
Cracking me open
Before greedily lapping up the yolk.

With Whom I Played

I went to town again today
Saw a thing consuming pavement space.
There was a hat, some random coins.
Plastic people scurried by
A chattering torrent pouring past.

I went to town again today
Watched a flower struggle from a crack.
It turned a feeble bloom towards the light.
No one marvelled at the sight
All people saw was black and white.

I went to town again today
Mixed with the Pharisees on Saturday.
Realised I was just the same.
A moral pygmy without shame
A busted flush in life's poker game.

I went to town again today
Balked at a wild man long gone grey.
Lost inside a matted beard
A playground friend from long ago
An ageing face without a home.

Without Hope

I honey the hemlock chalice
Drink a bitter distillation
That numbs my feet
Climbs the ladder of my spine.

Completing the work
Capturing on canvas
Brush-bristle rough
The raiment of my pain

I smear bright pigments
Into a raw retablo
Whilst the Sybil sings
Days of future past.

Violence of the Painting

Leaving smears of consciousness
Across a canvass
I capture the essence
Of human-snail hybrids.

Deformed mouths scream
At the injustice of death
Biting their escape
Through layers of paint.

Stabbing brush strokes
Poke holes in reality
Demanding a visceral response
From the central nervous system.

My restless eyes
Dart from left to right
As a new hell takes shape
In my pumpkin-head.

Vaulting

Time is consumed in an expansive maw
Candles illuminate heavenly grace
Beneath grandiose vaults of pious space.

Extravagance incarnate, unyielding walls,
Repose, let divine silence call
Amid the overwhelming splendour.

Lighting a candle with earnest thoughts
I entreat God with reckless candour
To crack your heart, the hardest stone of all.

Two Blind Mice

Hide in pint glasses
Hearing no evil
Seeing no evil
Speaking no evil.

Spawning introversion.
Chasing our tails
Round spilled truths
One molecule thick.

True Colours

A smiling image refracts
Through my neural net

Across seven million cones
And a hundred million rods.

An intimate moment
Captured and stored

With all the fidelity
Of a mechanical eye.

Springtime at the waiting room

Spring spreads its wings
Outside the waiting room.
Icicles dissolve
People thaw out
And unfurl their arms
Remembering what it's like
To live and love.

The sky clears its throat
And coughs out clouds.
Daffodils erupt
Through broken soil
Trains ply to and fro
Spitting out passengers
Engulfing waifs and strays.

Spring illuminates the fields.
Empty minutes pass
The hour glass
Re-fills itself with sand.
Sunlight pierces the realm
Of battered dreams
And promises warmth
A train, a life to catch

Keep customer informed
Quality assurance
A final thought;

Challenge the system:

Bet you can't
Put an egg
In your mouth
Without cracking it.

Roll-call of the Platitudes

Going the extra mile
Blue sky thinking;
Going forwards.

Customer satisfaction
Consumer delight;
Customer thrilled.

Meeting targets
Head count challenge;
Take the kings shilling?

Lead-to-sales
Angry-bird-manager;
Knitted brow, inefficient.

Touching base
Care survey;
Safe to speak up.

New computer
Multi-tasking;
Right first time

Drilled through cable
Service outage;
Claim for damages

Ball park figure
Colleagues figure;
Major disruption

San Francisco

With flowers in your hair
As if you are headed

For San Francisco
Or somewhere to the west

You beat your tambourine
Tapping out the rhythm of love.

As the darkening forest sighs
Your feet kiss the earth

Beneath the sacred tree
Within the secret grove.

Far away the sun sets over
The Pacific In shades of Gold.

Proverbs

Of Snow

When snow has fallen thick and deep
It is impossible to discern individual flakes;
But still they remain.

Of Longing

Never look back
Over a shoulder
Never try to recall
The perfume
Of her summer dress.

Of the Past Tense

Here I hid from you
Seven summers past
And wrote of love
Terrified of the same.

Of Reassessment

Remembering how it was
Because it matters;
Because it doesn't matter.

Precious Memories

I know I will forget your face
Although fighting

The thief called time
Every inch of the way.

Binding precious memories
With cords around my heart

I'll treasure them happily
Until the passing years betray

And you drift just out of reach
Becoming a beautiful dream

Warm, fuzzy, indistinct.

Passing Likeness

Exhaustion pulls me
Downwards, inwards;

Folding me in sleep;
A human origami.

A fleeting dream
Draws your face

Into a passing likeness
Until the waking hour

Comes like a thief
Stealing you away;

Silently and unannounced.

Parody of the Self

The image in the mirror
Leaks indifference.

That old thing staring back
Glass eyed and hollow.

Seeking a rope to climb
And leave this face

The introspective paints
A picture of itself
It christens "parody".

Once, Twice

It's so simple;
All I have to do is press once, twice,
And you appear smiling through a flat display.

So near;
I can reach out, extend a finger,
Touch an image, trace a smile.

Time retreats;
Memories kick inside, stretching the walls of my heart;
My eyes quarter the glass recreating the past.

Time retreats;
We're strolling together; a gentle breeze ripples your hair
I feel the sun on the back of my neck, inhale sea breezes.

Time retreats;
It's summertime, a train, a beach, good food;
The convivial fruity pop of wine corks.

It's so simple;
All I have to do is press once, twice;
Love coalesces on a screen.

Moon Crossed Lovers

Frost adorns your eyelids
Silvers your tongue.

Far more desirable;
The ascetic kiss of the moon.

Moai Hava

I can no longer see the waves
Or hear a seagull's cry
Rain has etched my pitted shell
None travelled so as I.

No longer with my brethren
Righteous men of stone
A weathered basalt curio
Lost, out of place, alone.

No tribal drums to pierce the night
And wake me from my sleep
Nor gifts from men, or deference
No observances to keep.

People hurry on to other sights
More interesting than I
Left hoping for a ship to come
And sail me back in time.

They ignore my brooding ugliness
Forgotten and forlorn
As I strain towards the rising sun
Volcanic, black of form.

For centuries I have longed for home
A voiceless abductee
An ageing, tired monolith
Still praying for release.

Please mark my final stand
Have pity in your heart
For this parody that once knew love;
A forgotten work of art.

Marbled Soul

I approach an icon
Quieten her lips with a kiss.

Her flawless skin pricks my heart
Devotion is the order of the day.

If there is pity in her chiselled eyes
The inadequate cannot reciprocate.

If there is love in her marbled soul
It is poorly requited.

Maple Leaves

She loosened the band and her hair fell
Like a red waterfall
Like fire tumbling over her shoulders

And in that moment my heart ran free
Through ancient forests
Through carpets of fallen leaves

She loosened the band and her hair fell
Unfettered across the curve of her neck

And she flicked her head
Her fiery hair describing an arc
Like an autumnal goddess

Her hair, red as a maple leaf
Promising the open skies of the wilderness
Her eyes as deep as the forest

She loosened the band and her hair fell
Wild and untamed
And I raised my head and howled to the moon.

Love Sarcophagus

She sings lullabies
To a half man, half experiment
Cocooned in her sterile womb.

Feeding on me feet first
I am reduced to slivers
On a glowing screen.

In a hemispherical sarcophagus
Seduced by metallic mantras
My senses depart one by one.

On this icy slab where time dies
Sound and vision fail;
Only love remains.

As I drift beneath her cloudless sky
She repeats over and again;
"I love you, I love you, I love you".

Drawn deep into her womb
She unlocks corporeal secrets
Croons a song of deconstruction.

Browsing my library of cells
Downloads her conclusions;
A high definition revelation.

She chants;

"Acknowledge the divine
This life is but a passing dream.
Rejoice in solitude without end;
Dance when the metal moon is high."

Locust Woman

The locust woman ate
Until my ribcage showed.
I had played with fire
Touched her flesh, been burned;
The hunter had become the hunted.

Kingdom of the Saguaro

When you have finished your sojourn
In the distant lands of summer rain

I will be here waiting, an ageing sentinel
Presiding over a thorn strewn kingdom

When, eventually, you decide to return
Use the old familiar opening in my chest

Lodge in the space where sap once rose,
In the deepest emptiness of my being.

I will enfold you with arms outstretched
Myriad spines clawing at the desert air

Uncertain roots grasping at shifting sand
That slips between them as once you did.

Whenever you need a safe haven
I will always welcome you home.

I am an echo chamber for love
You are an unquenchable thirst.

Kernel

Fluttering against the glass
Still he beats his wings
After long and fallow years
On the outside looking in.

A lonely, frightened mocking bird
With gold dust on his tongue
Carrying the burden
Of an imagined Midas touch.

So much to say, so little time
He would sing for you
Bring precious stones, a holly wreath
Things borrowed, old and blue.

It's bitter on the margins
The brittle edge of time
In deepest dark the brightest stars
Gleam in solitude divine.

Within this darkest hour
A kernel only night can bring
He awaits the cusp of sunrise
When he'll catch your eye and sing.

Irresolute Kiss

Ignoring setbacks I worked tirelessly
Determinedly inching my way towards
The epicentre of your disinterest.

Eventually I got my wish, we touched,
And I experienced the resigned
Indifference of an irresolute kiss.

Hubris

I would be a lark
Ascending out of sight

Lost in foolish hubris,
To celebrate myself.

Hollow Woman

Into her loving self she folds
Becomes a secret holy grail
Dives into the thin necked tube
Half buried between rolling hills.

Performs tricks for rich voyeurs
Unfurls a wanton inner sail
Makes a puzzle of her limbs
Sweet sanctuary for one and all.

If she were mine to have and hold
A harbour when all others fail
I'd sheath the love that I extrude
And not rely on bitter pills.

Henri Chapelle

These mute rows
Bear Testimony
To the passer-by
The far from home.

A choir of souls
Bridges the years
Across silent fields
Rows and rows.

Names and flowers,
Epitaphs;
"Thank you Dad"
Too brief a life.

All hitting home
The hurt and pain
Despite the years
Old scars remain.

This life of ease
By salt tears pricked
Our itinerary;
A small box ticked.

Ghost Child at the Window

Waving goodbye
The ghost child
Pulls away
To eternity
Teddy bear in hand.

The watcher
Knows the fate
Of the clanking train
The lies behind
"Resettlement".

Knows the final
Resting place
Of innocence;
That many years removed
Can still tear at the walls
Of a living heart.

Futility

As futile as caressing a rock
Making love to a stone
Or trying to thaw an iceberg
With my bare hands.

Foolish Hart

With a flailing, broken antler
Snapped at rutting time
Incanting ever upward
Toward Artemis shrine.

I never meant to hurt you
But my aim was straight and true.
The gods have reached their verdict
They dictate from depth of void.

Making all provision
Giving everything I could
I squandered heroism
In dark and tangled woods.

I battled to protect you
With confidence and pride
Now wounded and rejected
There's an arrow in my side.

Life has lost its meaning
The cycle is complete
Strength and false nobility
Lie wasted at your feet.

Foolish hart turned quarry
A moving target for your bow
Pierced for my transgressions
Reduced to carrion for crows.

Colour drains to black and white
As I struggle to recall
Why I sacrificed virility
Romanced this bruising fall?

I hope that you are happy
Beyond the touch of any man
I will deny my love, forget you,
In every way I can.

Flight of a Swallow

A bitter wind bites
The grey sky cracks
Across a frozen scene.

People perch
On battered stools
Drinking coffee

Recovering
From peace on earth
And mercy mild.

Who would imagine
A swallow flying up
From deepest Africa

Could make its home here
Beneath the eaves
A few short months from now?

Flavours of Blue

I smell the gnawing cold
Taste bitter shades of blue
Around my hollow heart
A dark miasma pools.

All spark of interest fades
Adopts unfamiliar hues
The cock it crows three times
I abandon hope of you.

Not wanting to be bold
Never taking higher ground
Fragile imagery breaks down
No shining path is found.

I swim against the tide
Even as the siren calls
Devotion mocks the self
Crowns the king of fools.

Your footfall quickly fades
Words hang in silent air
Illegitimate delusions
Concede to mute despair.

I meditate your absence
Shining angel unaware;
The finest of heart surgeons
Cannot fashion a repair.

Elusive Gold

The importance of the hour
Completely passed her by.

A mystery remained
Just beyond his grasp.

Words stalled;

And the pure gold
They might have shared

Lodged in their throats
Unspoken to the last.

Elder Gods

Once we held hands with the elder gods
Looked up to them for guidance
Comfort, warmth, food;
A straggling, querulous brood.

The day came for us to break stride
The elder gods were redundant
Left behind in the flow of passing years
To be visited on Sunday afternoons.

We watched them slowly ageing.
Now stooped and grey
Never wanting to make a fuss
They took the way of the stiff upper lip.

Holding hands with the elder gods again
The circle is complete;
Now we are the ones looking down
Exercising power of attorney.

Drone

He files from bloom to bloom
Collecting sweetest memories
Weighed down by myriad thoughts
To write this sad soliloquy;

Words to commemorate
The golden nectar of her kiss
And fantasize a different life
A better world than this.

Despite his finest waggle dance
She looked the other way
Ignoring heartfelt overtures
Made on a summer's day.

The neat honeycomb he fashioned
All the subtle hints he made
Were not enough to woo her love
Now all his cards are played.

Should he survive the wintertime
And live to fly again
"Beware the loveliest bloom of all"
Will be his sad refrain.

Drink Dissection

The body curio
Tilts its head
And swallows
Wondering how

The sectioned muscles
Would appear
In an exhibition
Or a glass jar
For all to see.

The pen moves faster
Ink unravels
Scaring the page
With spider trails
And amputations.

Driftwood Wreathes

A bell tolls, a seagull cries
For an audience of one.
Grey and melancholic clouds
Roll down to restless seas.

Summer has long flown its nest
The trees have shed their leaves.
Our golden beach is empty now
Clothed in driftwood wreathes.

If moments could be lived again
What different paths we'd take.
The sun has set on Shangri-la;
Across our cold and empty bed.

Distance

Taking time out to diligently meditate
Your persistent absence
I raise yet another glass to the mystery.

My fingers gently stroke images
Taken before false pride held sway
Caress a teardrop-spattered screen.

Dios de los Muertes

With a rattle of bones
The disappeared
Reproach the living.

Under fresh tilled sod
An anonymous
Mobile rings and dies.

A face on a poster smiles
But isn't true to life.
A mother weeps, a father cries.

Another disappearance
Logged on yellowing pages;
To be swept under a rug
Of government indifference.

2016

Here I sit
On the hair lip
Of the bowels of
The earth.

A strange
Vantage point;
Watching reality
Touching the ground.

Pondering serious things;
As my life force drains
Into the offertory bowl
Of a hopeless dream.

1989

An announcement comes;
The Berlin wall has fallen
Love will break out
Three years from now
And demand a kiss
From an ocean of faces
Currently indistinguishable.

1976

Long hot excuses.
I didn't respond
To decent advances

Or sow the future
On the carpet
Of a three story
Town house.

I'm sorry now;
Forty years later.
Sorry I couldn't
Stretch out a hand
And touch reality.

1946

Genius gives birth
To considered ugliness.

Asked why
The meat hangs
In Smithfield market
An umbrella
Presides over
Bared teeth and
Railing screams

Why split cattle
Parade their ribs
Or a milk-white
Statue pushes
Through a veil
Into nothingness

You reply;
"Because I want to.....
I want to capture reality;
Give it a new form"

Before adding;

"Drink up old chap,
Drink up;
And tonight
We'll scar the canvass together".

Dates for the Diary

<u>1916</u>

A flare rises
The whistles blow
We'll stroll this one
Away lads go!

The thundering guns
Old London hears;
We seeds stride out
Barbed wire cleared.

Chalk-white fields
Where poppies grow
Names and crosses
Row on row

The flower of youth
A simple prayer
An awful truth
For all lain bare.

The end is nigh
Old tenets fall
Innocence dies
For one and all.

Coming into Focus

Looking at the same picture
For ten years.
Leaning in slightly...

You lent in slightly
Coming into focus.

I admit the truth;
Trying to steal...

I was trying to steal your soul
Store it as data
Perhaps capture it for real.

I'd have gladly settled
For flesh and bone
But we were together apart...

Together apart
In pixel splendour.

This is the day I thought...

The day I thought would never end.

A perfect day
Without a cloud
The day I simply had to keep.

This is the day
A decade ago

When I focused the lens
And fingers trembling
Said "smile".

Coleopteran

To split the carapace and fly
This wretched shell, bent spine

And illuminate your sleep
With glowing chemicals;

Instead of languishing
Dusty on a lonely shelf.

With the mechanical rasp
Of a suitor's wings

I would soar beyond the obscenity
Of this puce and ailing frame

Pupate into the future
Reinvent the broken self.

Cities of Glass

A silent flash
Announces the fall
Of a star to earth.

The power of the sun
Boils rivers dry
Sucks life into the void.

Possesses souls
Fuses thoughts to glass
Leaves only shadows on the walls.

Cerberus

You withered on a vine
Vigilantly guarded
By the three headed dog
Of an ever-present past.

A tragedienne
Incarcerated in her dingy cell
Determined to disavow
Any would be keyholder.

Celestial Fall

I wished upon a shooting star
In its celestial fall
Hoped my love would unlock you
Prayers provide the key.

My heart burned in solitude
As it arced across your sky
Although worn upon these sleeves of mine
You never batted eye.

Love burned brightly for a season
Now darkness has returned
Mute silence blankets everything
All trace of where we were.

Cause for Complaint

"I'm sorry about that"
Was suffering from
Temporary insanity.

Didn't mean to be other than supine
The same recumbent person, resigned,
Punch-bag, pin cushion, easily abused.

"I'm sorry about that"
Didn't mean to have an opinion
That differed from your imperious position.

Expect customer service with a forced smile;
(A secret sag of resignation, phone ringing
Soft-phone, computer now, no chord);
Piping sound directly into tired ears.

Up again, day in day out
Trying to go the "extra mile"
And other management platitudes.

An accident, not a vocation.
Buckling under meaningless targets
Damn lies and statistics.

Calls come like a creeping barrage.
Waiting for my turn, a lottery;
Could be shouting or just mildly annoyed.

"I'm sorry about that"
Robotically trotting out the daily spiel
To one disembodied voice and all.

Catharsis

Radiant you enter the room
Long fingers briefly poise above

Hungry piano keys before
You play the notes of dreams.

Slender hands unlock
A joyful, easy cadence

A secret symphony hidden
Deep within your breast.

Notes swirl like birds released
To fill an empty room

Chords of aural sunshine
Dispelling winter's gloom.

Shy and bashful angel
Speaking music to my soul

You conjure sweet melodies
That salve unspoken longing.

Kiss me like the breeze
On a glorious summer's day

Leave a legacy of notes
A heart ascending like a lark.

Broken for You

God always kept count
Whilst we fingered rosary beads
For us revenants to sweat against.
He noted our insincere tears of repentance.

Body-Shaper

Human butterflies emerge from
Their changing room chrysalis

Into a realm of glass and mirror;
Scowls buried in I-pod hostility.

A zoology of sculpted muscle
Inhabits the labyrinth of weights.

Tired legs return having discharged
Their New Year's resolution.

Insistently tapping;
One, two, three, four
One, two, three, four...

The urgent serenade
Of the fairer sex;
A tempting call
To genuflection.

All enacted to
Faint radio strains
Of "love, love me do"
With harmonica.

Blue Nails

You rhythmically drum
Your nails on the desk
In ascending pitch

Insistently tapping;
One, two, three, four
One, two, three, four...

An office Goddess
Conjuring white horses
From the seas of an endless day.

My heart somersaults
Longing to be unfurled
To billow on swells of myth.

Aphrodite...
Insistently tapping;
One, two, three, four
One, two, three, four...

Conjuring dreams of love
Visions of pathways
Known only to the gods
Where pleasure hides.

The beat of my heart
Your fingers;
The vault of my longing
Your lips.

Beneath the Joshua tree

A chill wind thrashes leafless branches
Raindrops hurl themselves at glass.
Beneath the Joshua tree
Praying into a cloak of darkness
I try to reach the distant ear of God.

Asp and Dove

Side-winding on a moment
The emboldened tongue
Extrudes in snake-like form.

True love uncoils
A lingual spine
Gifts its pleasure storm.

Sloughs familiar skin
Skips a beat;
Asp hypnotises dove.

Impales us in surrender
On the forked tongued
Peaks of love.

Arid Evening

She ignores a casualty of drink
Sticking to the business side of things.

He hopes a volcano will erupt
Spewing forth love in all its glory.

Instead life's scribes and Pharisees
Impart acerbic judgement.

Further incoherence, she retreats;
Eros has fucked up.

Aphrodite won't pass the time of day
Not on this arid evening, anyway.

Altar of Petals

There is a new flower in the field
A lovelier bloom than all before.
She turns bright petals to the sun
Whilst her lover sings in gratitude.

No greater treasure can there be
Than heed the carpel's fertile call.
Sweet inner sanctum, holy ground
Love's fragrant altar of sacrifice.

All the Things

All the things I'd written for you
A final touch, a careless stroke
And everything is lost.

A screen full of emptiness remains
Lilly white, like my coward's heart
Pierced on a crown of words.

Irretrievable sentiments
Brimming with all the things
I never had the courage to say.

Ajar

I'm on the outside looking in
Watching as your footprints
On the shifting sands of time
Are washed away.

Intently listening from a distance
An ear pressed to the ground
I'm a wandering piece of flotsam
Lost and found.

I'm the face in the rear-view
The wreck upon your reef
Where once there was torment
And grinding of teeth.

I still reap the high tide
Of a golden summer past
An inadequate encounter
All too brief.

You tarried for a season
Passed your darkest hour
Now like a timid vixen
Gone to ground

You've found your own way home
Such a beautiful thief
Not troubling to close the heart
You left ajar.

Ageing Attractions

An outbreak of sex
A decade ago
Would have been nice.

Across the chipped table
Or on the careworn
Parquet floor.

Tired smiles
Mutual weariness
A refilled glass.

Forgive the intrusion of desire.
The brief interruption
Of inappropriate thoughts.

Ouroboros

The journey began
Where we lost ourselves
And you touched my arm.

I truly lived in that moment
Comforted by the fingertips
That lightly caressed the thin
Separation of my sleeve.

Breech Birth

No one knew from whence he came
The Jackalope appeared one day
Leaping through a hole in time
Patchwork quilt, blood and slime.

Fashioned from unwanted parts
Mismatched mess, legs and arms
Thought himself as others taught
Often lying, sometimes caught.

Butt of jokes, envied one
Auto-erotic, prodigal son
Stay-at-home, seldom kissed
Bag of bones, rack of ribs.

Prim and proper, maladroit
Rising tide, King Canute
Philistine, bon viveur
Snappy dresser, mangy cur.

These are the tales of the Jackalope
Here he comes, there he goes!
Would be lover, can of worms
Horrid fellow, fragrant rose.

No one knew from whence he came
The Jackalope appeared one day
Leaping through a hole in time
Patchwork quilt, blood and slime.

Maple Leaves	46
Marbled Soul	47
Moai Hava	48
Moon Crossed Lovers	49
Once Twice	50
Parody of the Self	51
Passing Likeness	52
Precious Memories	53
Proverbs	54
San Francisco	55
Roll-call of the Platitudes	56
Springtime at the Waiting Room	58
True Colours	59
Two Blind Mice	60
Vaulting	61
Violence of the Painting	62
Without Hope	63
With Whom I Played	64
Yolk	65
The Beating Heart Metaphor	66

Dates for the Diary 21

Dios de los Muertes 26

Distance 27

Driftwood Wreathes 28

Drink Dissection 29

Drone 30

Elder Gods 31

Elusive Gold 32

Flavours of Blue 33

Flight of a Swallow 34

Foolish Hart 35

Futility 36

Ghost Child at the Window 37

Henry Chapelle 38

Hollow Woman 39

Hubris 40

Irresolute Kiss 41

Kernel 42

Kingdom of the Saguaro 43

Locust Woman 44

Love Sarcophagus 45

Contents

Breech Birth..1

Ouroboros..2

Ageing Attractions...3

Ajar...4

All the Things...5

Altar of Petals..6

Arid Evening...7

Asp and Dove...8

Beneath the Joshua Tree...9

Blue Nails..10

Body Shaper...12

Broken for You...13

Catharsis..14

Cause for Complaint..15

Celestial Fall...16

Cerberus..17

Cities of Glass..18

Coleopteran...19

Coming into Focus...20

Introduction

A keen traveller and hobbyist Mark was born in London and has spent his life in Essex.

He turned to poetry as a creative way of dealing with bereavement and what started as an exploration into emotional expression quickly turned into a passion for the written word.

Inspiration comes from his own life, those he meets and from artists and writers, among whom favourites are Leonard Cohen, Emily Dickinson and Frida Kahlo.

This book gathers together selected short poems drawn from an extensive body of work written over the last decade.

Colchester, Essex, England
February 2024

Dedication

To the mythical creature in us all

I would like to thank my wife Liz
for her help and support
in selecting and editing these poems.

Mark B. Harris

Copyright © Mark B. Harris

Mark B. Harris has asserted his right under
Section 77 of the Copyright, Designs and Patents Act 1988
To be identified as the author of this work.

ISBN: 979 8876 7 7597 9

Jackalope

Mark B. Harris

Ariadne's Thread Publishing

ariadnesthreadpublishing@gmail.com